MUSIC

Urban Entrepreneur: Music

Scobre Educational
2255 Calle Clara
La Jolla, CA 92037

Scobre Operations & Administration
42982 Osgood Road
Fremont, CA 94539

www.scobre.com
info@scobre.com

Scobre Educational publications may be purchased for
educational, business, or sales promotional use.

Cover and layout design by Jana Ramsay
Copyedited by Renae Reed
Some photos by Getty Images

ISBN: 978-1-61570-951-9 (E-Book)
ISBN: 978-1-61570-887-1 (Hard Cover)
ISBN: 978-1-61570-873-4 (Soft Cover)

TABLE OF CONTENTS

Chapter 1
The Songbird

Nestled between some of the United States' most historic monuments lies The National Mall, a large, open-area park in Washington, D.C. On January 21, 2013, this distinguished strip of land was crammed with eager onlookers, gathered to witness the swearing in of Barack Obama to his second term as our nation's president.

Wrapped in heavy winter coats, people stamped their feet on the cold, hard ground, stuffed frigid hands deep into their pockets, and directed their attention toward a U.S. Capitol building draped in American flags.

A lone figure quietly and gracefully took center stage. She opened her mouth and her voice rose, softly at first, like a child waking from slumber. Within seconds, it soared confidently, lifting above the marching drums, the trumpets, the violins. Then it descended, coming to rest upon a tree's high limb. The crowd erupted.

The power of song cannot be captured by words or symbols. It does not require explanation. A voice can travel directly to

The U.S. Capitol Building on Inauguration Day.

the core of our very beings. There are few voices on the planet capable of moving us as swiftly and as deeply as the one that belongs to Beyoncé Knowles.

The flight of the songbird known as Beyoncé began in the fourth largest city in the United States—Houston, Texas, a city rich with diverse cultural influences. Nowhere is Houston's rich diversity more clearly demonstrated than in its music scene. From rock and blues to hip hop, country, and Tejano (also

Beyonce puts her heart into "The Star-Spangled Banner."

known as Texan-Mexican music), Houston is a musical melting pot.

Beyoncé entered the Houston music scene when she joined the group Girl's Tyme. She was eight years old. It was as a member of this group that her incredible talent became apparent to her whole family and Beyoncé's music career became the family's mission. After Girl's Tyme was defeated on the nationally televised talent show "Star Search," Beyoncé's father quit his job in order to manage them. Her mother, a hair stylist and salon owner, volunteered her place of business as a rehearsal space. Needless to say, the family's investment in their daughter paid off.

By 1998 the group had changed their name to Destiny's Child and their debut self-titled album, *Destiny's Child,* had topped the charts. The group didn't slow down from there. With their second album, *The Writing's on the Wall*, they became one of the most successful music acts in the country. At the center of all the attention was Beyoncé, a star that reminded many of two R&B legends that came before her.

Born in Detroit, Michigan, in 1944, Diana Ross' career began at a time when only a few African-American females (such as Billie Holiday and Etta James) had found a path to success in the music business. Racism made a career in the public eye a tremendous mountain to climb. Despite the odds, Ross rose from a department store clerk to Motown's brightest star. To this day, she is still recording music and touring the globe. In 2006, Beyoncé garnered critical acclaim for her portrayal of a character based on a young Diana Ross in the hit film "Dreamgirls."

In 2009, the Guinness Book of World Records bestowed the title of "Most Awarded Female Act of All Time" to Whitney Houston. Like Beyoncé, Whitney's music career began when she was very young.

Cousin to Dionne and Dee Dee Warwick and honorary niece to legendary R&B and soul singer Aretha Franklin, Whitney began performing professionally when she was 14. In 1992, her career expanded to the silver screen with the smash hit "The Bodyguard." The soundtrack to the movie sold over a million copies in just one week, and Whitney's signature song, "I Will Always Love You," became the best-selling single by a female artist of all time.

Like those remarkable women, Beyoncé knew that her talents as a solo vocalist and

Aretha Franklin, the original Queen of Soul, sang at President Obama's first inauguration ceremony in 2008.

actress could take her places that Destiny's Child could not hope to go. Beyoncé needed space to spread her wings, to soar beyond the music industry and into the rarefied air of cultural idols.

In 2013, by the time the year was a mere 35 days old, Beyoncé had sung at a presidential inauguration and performed at the Super Bowl. The little girl from Houston, Texas, who lit up stages as a member of Girl's

Beyoncé performs before hundreds of millions of viewers around the world at Super Bowl XLVII.

Tyme had grown into the kind of superstar that only comes along once or twice in a generation. But without Whitney and Diana, there would be no Beyoncé. Without Etta James, Billie Holiday, Ella Fitzgerald, Aretha Franklin, and Nina Simone, there would have been no Whitney or Diana. Beyoncé can only hope that history will one day place her beside the gifted and courageous women who paved the road for others to follow.

Chapter 2
The Business...Man

"I'm not afraid of dying, I'm afraid of not trying," Jay-Z professes in "Beach Song." For Jay-Z, "not trying" means more than not producing music. For Jay-Z, "trying" means taking big risks, it means knocking down barriers, it means that, in a society that too often rewards dishonesty, you stay true to your roots.

Raised in the Marcy Houses projects of Bedford-Stuyvesant, Brooklyn, Jay-Z's childhood was a struggle. When he was a teenager, a drug epidemic swept through urban New York like a plague. Life was

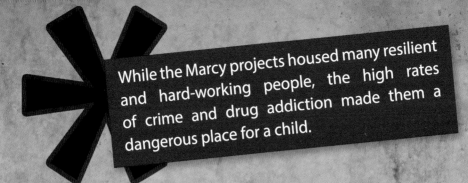

tremendously hard for any young man or woman simply trying to survive. Many could not escape a life of addiction and crime; those who survived would be forever changed.

Suffering doesn't necessarily make you stronger, but in the case of Jay-Z and other hip hop artists like him, their frustration and anger served as the raw materials for creating something lasting and meaningful. They created a music that would speak to, and speak for, millions of America's voiceless poor.

The hip hop revolution officially began in 1982 when Bronx natives Grandmaster Flash and the Furious Five released "The Message." Its lyrics spoke of a population cut off from opportunity, of the anger and frustration that artists like Stevie Wonder and Marvin Gaye had been singing about in their hit 1970s songs

Grandmaster Flash is credited with having invented the "crossfader," a switch that allows DJs to go from one record after another without a break in the music.

"Living for The City" and "What's Going On?" But the lyrics of "The Message," spoken instead of sung, conveyed an anger that could not be overlooked. There was no pretty melody, softening the blunt power of the words. "Don't push me cause I'm close to the edge," was not so much a threat as it was a rallying cry.

In 1984, Russell Simmons and Rick Rubin launched the Def Jam Recording label and a new chapter in the history of urban America began to be written. Def Jam recording artists Run-D.M.C. and Public Enemy were the foundation upon which a new empire was constructed. These groups would tell the truth about their world as they saw it. Soon enough, truth telling would become infectious. Young

men and women all over the country would be adding their voices to the growing chorus.

Shawn Carter had always been a musical child. His mother, Gloria, recalled him banging out drum patterns on the kitchen table and driving everyone in the apartment crazy. When she finally broke down and bought him a boombox, Shawn began writing lyrics and freestyling. People in the neighborhood, respectful of his skills, called him "Jazzy," the name that evolved into Jay-Z. Gaining respect as a rapper in Bed-Stuy, a city that produced such hip hop greats as the Notorious B.I.G. and Mos Def may have been harder than anywhere else on

In addition to his jaw-dropping rhymes, Mos Def is an accomplished actor.

the planet. Jay-Z's was one of many voices battling to be heard.

By the early 1990s, Jay-Z was appearing on stage with established hip hop talents and having rap battles with LL Cool J. He won rap battle after rap battle, emerging as one of New York's hottest young MCs. He started appearing on albums released by other New York rappers such as Big Daddy Kane and Ja Rule.

In 1996, Jay-Z released his debut album, *Reasonable Doubt*. The album established him as a major force in hip hop. Then, while grieving over the loss of his high school friend and hip hop peer, Notorious

B.I.G., Jay-Z recorded and released *In My Lifetime, Vol. 1*. The album went platinum and Jay-Z became more than one of the country's biggest hip hop acts; he became one of the biggest music acts period.

Jay-Z cannot be easily defined. "I'm not a businessman, I'm a business… man," he's proclaimed. His career as a rapper, record producer, clothing designer, and part owner of the NBA's Brooklyn Nets certainly backs up that assertion. Jay-Z is a true urban entrepreneur, one of the most dramatic

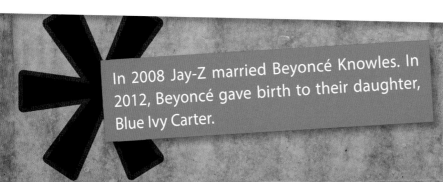

In 2008 Jay-Z married Beyoncé Knowles. In 2012, Beyoncé gave birth to their daughter, Blue Ivy Carter.

rags-to-riches stories imaginable. His story is one of success in the face of struggle and loss. But it is also a story of ambition and innovation, of swagger and pride. Just like the music he helped develop, Jay-Z continues to evolve.

Chapter 3
Nashville's Newest Queen

In 2005, a tall fifteen-year-old girl with blond hair, blue eyes, and zero trace of stage fright sat down amongst a group of seasoned musicians in Nashville, Tennessee's legendary Bluebird Café. Located near the heart of Nashville's Music Row, Bluebird is truly one of a kind. In its music-in-the-round setting, singers and songwriters take turns playing their tunes and accompanying one another for a small crowd of just over 100 people. In this modest setting, record executives from numerous recording labels are regular attendees and country music icons like Kathy Mattea and Garth Brooks were discovered.

The tall fifteen-year-old girl played her heartfelt songs with the same poise, skill, and honesty she had since she was a child. For such a young performer, the road traveled to this point had already been

Musicians and fans nestle into the cozy confines of the Bluebird Café for a country throwdown.

Taylor signs autographs for devoted fans.

strenuous. But this teenager showed no hint of fatigue. She demonstrated the talent and depth that has since inked her name into the history books and taken her to the top of the music industry.

In 2005, Taylor Swift was not merely presenting herself to recording executives in the hopes of getting signed to a record label. What Taylor was attempting to do at the Bluebird Café was sell people on an idea: a teenage girl could write and record her own songs and people across the country would want to buy them. To most country music executives, this idea seemed far-fetched. But to Taylor, writing was just as important as performing. Her desire was not to sing songs to large crowds. Her desire was to tell those crowds the story of her life as she lived it.

As long as there has been country

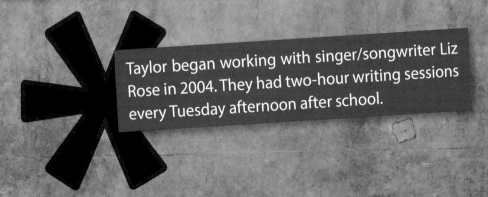

Taylor began working with singer/songwriter Liz Rose in 2004. They had two-hour writing sessions every Tuesday afternoon after school.

music, there have been country musicians, spilling their guts for a shot at recognition. Some have sought fame and fortune—an appearance on WSM radio's Grand Ole Opry, the longest-running radio show in U.S. history, could make a musician a household name overnight. Others merely desired to make a living, playing the music that they loved. Whatever their ambition, if a musician wanted to make a career in country music, there was one place they needed to be: Nashville, Tennessee.

Dubbed "Music City" in the early 20th century, Nashville has come to be known as "the songwriting capital of the world."

The intersection of Music Square East and Music Square North in the area known as "Music Row."

During the Great Depression, radio was one of the few sources of entertainment for people with no extra money for things like movies or restaurants. The Grand Ole Opry, broadcast out of Nashville, became an absolute sensation. Loyal listeners from 30 different states tuned their dials to WSM every Saturday night for a mix of country, bluegrass, folk, gospel, comedic

In addition to Taylor Swift, artists such as Kings of Leon, The Black Keys, Michael McDonald, Keb' Mo', Sheryl Crow, Paramore, Hot Chelle Rae, and Jack White have made Nashville their home.

performances, and skits. Making his first appearance on Grand Ole Opry in 1946 was a guitar-picking genius named Chet Atkins.

A virtuosic musician and creator of what the media labeled the "Nashville Sound," Chet Atkins wrote, recorded, and produced music in the area now known as "Music Row" for decades. Without his innovations, Elvis Presley and rock and roll might have wiped out country music altogether. Instead,

Chet Atkins developed a sound that broadened country music's appeal, and helped preserve Nashville's standing in the music world.

During her Bluebird Café performance, Taylor caught the attention of a record executive, and in October of 2006, Big Machine Records released her debut album, *Taylor Swift*. *The New York Times* called it "a small

Taylor performing at Madison Square Garden in New York City.

Taylor playing before a crowd of 51,000 screaming fans in her home state of Pennsylvania.

masterpiece of pop-minded country," but it was Taylor's tireless self-promotion that made it a hit. She used the online social networking site Myspace to grow her fan base, appeared on the television version of "Grand Ole Opry," as well as "Good Morning America" and "TRL," and baked cookies for radio station programmers who played her music. Her hard work paid off. *Taylor Swift* has now sold nearly six million copies.

Taylor's subsequent albums *Fearless* and *Speak Now* have combined to sell over 14 million copies worldwide. She has expanded the appeal of country music and inspired countless teenage girls across the world to value their voices.

Taylor doesn't write for the masses; she writes for herself. But in her songs about struggling to fit into this world are the stories of millions of young girls who have experienced the same ups and downs. She brought country music into the 21st century using the same model that worked for country musicians for over a hundred years: write honestly about your life.

Chapter 4

American Idols

In the 1980s, the northwest side of Berkeley, California, was bleak and gray. In no way did it resemble the Berkeley that had become famous in the 1960s. Berkeley had once been a shining beacon of resistance, the place where political activists spoke out for free speech and 100,000 people marched in

Mario Savio being hauled away by campus police during a demonstration for free speech at UC Berkeley.

protest of the Vietnam War. But to a stranger passing through in the 1980s, Northwest Berkeley looked no different than any other industrial town: colorless and dull. Who could have predicted that from a landscape of warehouses, train tracks, and the city dump that punk rock, the music of rebellion and revolt, was about to be reborn?

924 Gilman Steet was established in 1986 by founders who cared deeply about bringing good music to the public. These founders had funny ideas about money and music. They believed that the two did not mix. Holding to this principle, they decided that 924 Gilman would be cooperatively run. If you wanted to see shows, you had to

become a member. To become a member, all you had to do was pay $2.00 a year and follow four basic rules: No drugs. No alcohol. No violence. No racism. Follow those rules and you were free to enjoy all the punk rock your eardrums could handle.

From the street, 924 Gilman looked like a beat-up old post office without the American flag. But the building's insides teemed with life. Between walls covered in graffiti, masses of frustrated teens and young adults needing a break from a world that expected them

Bands such as Green Day, AFI, The Offspring, Operation Ivy, and The Dead Kennedys all performed at 924 Gilman.

to be polite, play nice, and not cause a scene jumped and danced and banged their heads to the aggressive, angry, surging beat of the best punk rock the Bay Area had to offer. It was beneath Gilman's exposed wooden rafters and before a sweating, seething mass of bodies that the punk rock idols known as Green Day earned their stripes.

Northern California boys Billie Joe Armstrong and Mike Dirnt formed their first band, a four-piece group called Sweet Children, when they were fifteen. Two years later the group had whittled themselves down to a trio, changed their name to Green Day, and released their first album entitled *1,000 Hours*. The sound was raw, energetic and distinctly punk. Inspired heavily by English punk rock legends The Clash and American godfathers of punk The Ramones, *1,000 Hours* helped solidify the Bay Area's reputation as the heart of punk's rebirth. Green Day continued to evolve, adding drummer Tré Cool and releasing *Kerplunk*. The album confirmed their standing as one of California's top punk acts along with bands like The Offspring and Rancid.

Before releasing their third album, *Dookie*, Green Day signed with Reprise Records. Signing with a major record label meant a wider audience and a chance to make a lot more money. But the deal would not come

Tré, Billie Joe, and Mike goof around backstage at Madison Square Garden.

without a price. 924 Gilman did not allow bands that had signed with major record labels to play their club. To move away from the club that had nurtured them meant taking the chance that they might never be welcomed back.

Believing in their ability to stay true to their punk roots, Green Day made the decision to take their music to a bigger stage. Whatever kind of change they prepared themselves for, there was no way they could have foreseen what they were to become.

Green Day's third album, *Dookie*, sold over

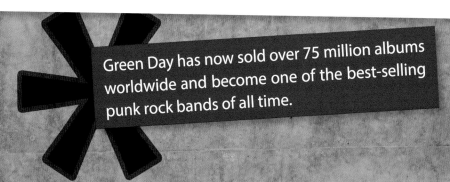

Green Day has now sold over 75 million albums worldwide and become one of the best-selling punk rock bands of all time.

16 million copies. The band won countless awards and went on world tours, playing in front of crowds as large as 100,000 people. In 2004, they reinvented themselves with the rock opera *American Idiot*. It would prove to be their biggest hit yet. *American Idiot* was turned into a musical and became a smash

hit on Broadway. Green Day became one of the most famous music acts in the world.

In a scene dominated by teenagers, Green Day is still at the top after 25 years. Given their past, it's impossible to predict where the band will go next. But fans can rest assured of one thing: Green Day will never relent.

At a concert in San Antonio, Texas Billie Joe encourages the crowd to sing along.